NO LONG
SEATTLI

D0788423

UU   2019

By

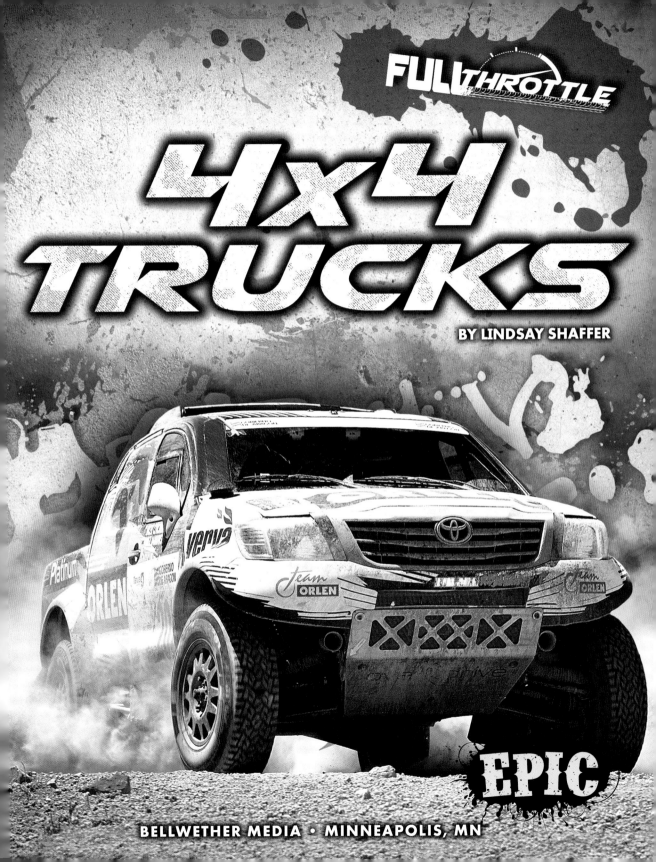

FULL THROTTLE

4X4 TRUCKS

BY LINDSAY SHAFFER

EPIC

BELLWETHER MEDIA • MINNEAPOLIS, MN

EPIC

EPIC BOOKS are no ordinary books. They burst with intense action, high-speed heroics, and shadows of the unknown. Are you ready for an Epic adventure?

This edition first published in 2019 by Bellwether Media, Inc.

No part of this publication may be reproduced in whole or in part without written permission of the publisher. For information regarding permission, write to Bellwether Media, Inc., Attention: Permissions Department, 6012 Blue Circle Drive, Minnetonka, MN 55343.

Library of Congress Cataloging-in-Publication Data

Names: Shaffer, Lindsay, author.
Title: 4x4 Trucks / by Lindsay Shaffer.
Other titles: 4 x 4 trucks | Four by four trucks
Description: Minneapolis, MN : Bellwether Media, Inc., 2019. | Series: Epic.
   Full Throttle | Includes bibliographical references and index. | Audience:
   Ages 7-12. | Audience: Grades 2 to 7.
Identifiers: LCCN 2018002176 (print) | LCCN 2018008077 (ebook) | ISBN
   9781626178694 (hardcover : alk. paper) | ISBN 9781681036168 (ebook)
Subjects: LCSH: Four-wheel drive trucks–Juvenile literature.
Classification: LCC TL230.5.F6 (ebook) | LCC TL230.5.F6 S488 2019 (print) | DDC 629.223/2–dc23
LC record available at https://lccn.loc.gov/2018002176

Text copyright © 2019 by Bellwether Media, Inc. EPIC and associated logos are trademarks and/or registered trademarks of Bellwether Media, Inc. SCHOLASTIC, CHILDREN'S PRESS, and associated logos are trademarks and/or registered trademarks of Scholastic Inc., 557 Broadway, New York, NY 10012.

Editor: Christina Leaf   Designer: Jeffrey Kollock

Printed in the United States of America, North Mankato, MN

TABLE OF CONTENTS

OFF-ROAD ADVENTURE!

Dirt and dust spray into the air. Tires scramble over the **rugged** land. The 4x4 truck hits a rough bump. The tires leave the ground! The truck lands and zooms ahead to continue the race.

The truck is nearing the finish line. The driver pushes the gas and roars into the lead.

He steers through a narrow path and powers up the final hill. His truck wins the race!

WHAT ARE 4x4 TRUCKS?

4x4 trucks are named for their four-wheel drive. They are called 4x4s for short. Four-wheel drive means the engine powers all four wheels. This helps 4x4 trucks drive **off-road**. It provides better **traction** and easier turning.

People use 4x4 trucks for jobs too tough for smaller cars. 4x4s can tow heavy objects, carry supplies, and drive on rough **terrain**.

GO BIG!
Many monster trucks are made from 4x4s.

Some people drive 4x4 trucks in races and **competitions**.

THE HISTORY OF 4x4 TRUCKS

The military first used 4x4s in the early 1900s. Soldiers drove 4x4s during World War I. They carried soldiers and weapons. During World War II, 4x4s gained even more popularity.

World War I

HORSE POWER

4x4 vehicles replaced horse-drawn carts for carrying supplies.

World War II

4x4 TIMELINE

Marmon-Herrington starts putting four-wheel drive in some Ford pickup trucks

1935

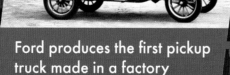

Ford produces the first pickup truck made in a factory

1925

1946

DODGE

Dodge Power Wagon becomes the first 4x4 truck built for everyday use

1974-79

Bob Chandler builds the first monster truck using a 4x4 pickup truck

In 1946, Dodge redesigned military 4x4s into everyday trucks. People used them for off-road work. Today, people drive 4x4 trucks for many reasons. Families use them for errands or camping trips. Farmers use them to haul materials.

PARTS OF A 4x4 TRUCK

The **chassis**, or base, of a 4x4 truck is made of steel bars. The body of the truck rests on top of the chassis. The wheels attach to the **axles** on the bottom.

SPLASH OF COLOR!

Drivers can paint their 4x4 trucks with bright colors and designs. Flames are a popular choice.

OFF-ROAD SAFETY

4x4 trucks often need special tires for mud, sand, snow, or ice.

A 4x4 needs a strong **suspension system**. This **absorbs** shock and helps keep the wheels on the ground. Without it, driving a 4x4 truck would be bumpy and unsafe.

IDENTIFY A 4x4 TRUCK

body

chassis

suspension system

axle

4x4 TRUCK COMPETITIONS

Some people race 4x4 trucks through **obstacle courses**. They compete for the best times on rocky, muddy trails.

obstacle course

mud bogging

Mud bogging is another 4x4 sport. Drivers compete to go the farthest through thick, slimy mud. They enjoy pushing their 4x4s to the limit!

GLOSSARY

absorbs—takes in

axles—bars attached to each wheel that make the wheels spin

chassis—the frame of a vehicle, usually made of steel bars

competitions—contests

obstacle courses—racetracks with special challenges

off-road—on trails or dirt roads

rugged—rough or rocky

suspension system—the system of springs, tires, and shocks that cushions a vehicle's ride

terrain—land

traction—the ability to grip a surface while moving

TO LEARN MORE

AT THE LIBRARY

Adamson, Thomas K. *Monster Trucks*. Minneapolis, Minn.: Bellwether Media, 2019.

Farndon, John. *Megafast Trucks*. Minneapolis, Minn.: Hungry Tomato, 2016.

Mack, Larry. *Toyota Tacoma*. Minneapolis, Minn.: Bellwether Media, 2019.

ON THE WEB

Learning more about 4x4 trucks is as easy as 1, 2, 3.

1. Go to www.factsurfer.com.

2. Enter "4x4 trucks" into the search box.

3. Click the "Surf" button and you will see a list of related web sites.

With factsurfer.com, finding more information is just a click away.

INDEX

The images in this book are reproduced through the courtesy of: Rodrigo Garrido, front cover, pp. 1, 4-5, 6, 7, 11, 14-15, 16-17; Dodge Media Center, pp. 8-9; Chevrolet, pp. 10, 19 (truck); Bettmann/ Getty Images, pp. 12, 15 (Bigfoot); IWM/ Getty Images, pp. 12-13; Michael Dwyer/ Alamy, p. 14; Chrysler Corp./ Wikipedia, p. 15 (Power Wagon); Ford Media Center, pp. 18-19; Etaphop Photo, p. 19 (suspension); Ake Apichai Chumsri, p. 19 (axle); Nachaliti, p. 20; Ovu0ng, pp. 20-21.